LIFE AND TIMES IN
ANCIENT
ROME

KINGFISHER
BOSTON

KINGFISHER

a Houghton Mifflin Company imprint
222 Berkeley Street
Boston, Massachusetts 02116
www.houghtonmifflinbooks.com

Based on material first published in the Sightseers series in 2000
This edition first published in 2007

2 4 6 8 10 9 7 5 3 1

1TR/0607/TIMS/(MA)/14OMA/C

Copyright © Kingfisher Publications Plc 2007

Written and edited by: Conrad Mason, Jonathan Stroud
Coordinating editors: Caitlin Doyle, Stephanie Pliakas
Consultant: David Nightingale
Production controller: Aysun Ackay
DTP manager: Nicky Studdart
DTP operator: Claire Cessford

Illustrations by: Inklink Firenze and Kevin Maddison

LIBRARY OF CONGRESS CATALOGING-IN-PUBLICATION DATA
has been applied for.

ISBN 978-0-7534-6151-8

Printed in China

Contents

The city of Rome

At the time of its settlement, Rome was not much more than a few farmers' houses on an Italian hillside, but it grew to become the head of the largest empire the world had ever seen. Rome ruled over people from places as far apart as Great Britain and Egypt, but the city remained the heart of the empire, home to one million people at the height of its power. But while riches poured into the city, almost one fourth of the population was unemployed and relied on free grain.

◁ By A.D. 128 the empire was so big that the emperor, Hadrian (A.D. 76–138), spent most of his time away from Rome, protecting the empire's boundaries. This book is about the city of Rome in Hadrian's time.

According to legend, Rome was founded in 753 B.C. by Romulus and Remus. It was said that they were brought up by a wolf.

For centuries, Rome was ruled by a senate of the most important men. The eagle became the symbol of Rome.

Rome's first rival was the African city of Carthage. In 218 B.C. it invaded Rome with elephants, but was defeated.

rostrum

senate house

The city's spiritual heart was the forum, or marketplace. When Rome was just a village, its people met in this open space to trade and discuss politics. By the time of Hadrian, the old square had been built up with large temples and political memorials, and the markets had moved elsewhere. The senate house stood next to the forum, but the real center of power was the emperor's palace nearby.

◁ Rome was a city of extremes. It was full of spacious palaces and public buildings, but it was extremely crowded, with very narrow streets. A tiny elite was staggeringly rich, but one third of Rome's inhabitants were slaves.

For 250 years after beating Carthage, Rome's disciplined armies conquered all of the lands around the Mediterranean Sea.

A great general, Julius Caesar (100–44 B.C.), took power and ruled Rome alone, but he was murdered by the senators.

Caesar's adopted son Augustus (63 B.C.–A.D. 14) took over from the senate. He was the first of many emperors.

5

Transportation

The Romans needed excellent transportation and communication in order to keep control over their empire, so they constructed a vast network of long, straight highways. This road system was built by the Roman army and stretched over more than 30,000 mi. (50,000km) in total. It was possible to travel from one end of the empire to the other in 100 days on horseback. Inside Rome itself it was easy to get lost—none of the thousands of winding streets had names or numbers.

△ The Tiber river in Rome was a major transportation route, with merchant ships sailing to and from the coast, bringing grain, wine, and other supplies.

▷ Romans built roads with long-lasting foundations. A flat layer of sand went on the bottom, with layers of stone and gravel above. The road was topped with paving stones, which were curved to let rain run off. Engineers had tools to keep the road straight so that journeys would take as little time as possible.

▽ With no street names, citizens found their way around Rome by using temples and statues as landmarks.

◁ Wealthy Romans had teams of slaves to carry them around the city.

In Rome the roads were covered with mud, garbage, and sewage. Raised sidewalks and steppingstones helped people keep their feet dry, and the wealthy traveled by sedan chair. Streets were busy even at night, as traders with noisy, slow-moving carts were only allowed inside the city at dusk. Citizens who went out at night would often take slaves with them for protection—muggers and thieves were common.

Clothing

To a Roman it was very important to have the latest hairstyle and clothing. Fashions changed often. For instance, Roman men were clean-shaven until the emperor Hadrian started a trend for having beards. Men usually wore tunics, but had robes called togas for special occasions.

△ Rich women had personal slaves to shape their hair into elaborate styles. This could take all morning. Others wore wigs made from the hair of foreign slaves. Blond hair from German women was seen as very exotic.

◁ Romans used various tools to help improve their looks. These included combs, hairpins, tweezers for plucking hairs, and even small spoons for scooping wax out of ears.

▽ Both men and women wore jewelry, including brooches to close their cloaks. The rich had rings, bracelets, and necklaces made out of gold or silver, while the poor had bronze jewelry. The finest pieces were set with precious stones from the farthest parts of the empire.

◁ For women, a pale face was a sign of status. Poor women had rough, red faces from working outside. Many Romans used creams made of chalk, flour, and lead to whiten their skin.

Wealthy men showed their status by wearing long tunics. Poor men and slaves had short tunics that were more practical and gave their legs more freedom as they worked. A fashionable Roman woman took great care with her clothes. She would wear an ankle-length woolen undertunic, with a colorful embroidered dress, or stola, on top. This was made out of wool, cotton, or silk.

Food and drink

Rich Romans enjoyed an unending array of exotic delicacies—from stuffed dormouse to ostrich and flamingo. The poor made do with grain boiled into porridge and mixed with cheap foods like eggs and cheese. For these Romans, meat was a rare treat. Wine mixed with water was the usual drink for all citizens, both rich and poor. It was considered vulgar to drink undiluted wine. Cena, or dinner, was the biggest meal of the day.

△ For most Romans, breakfast and lunch were light meals that could be eaten quickly while standing up.

△ Roman cooks used strong, spicy sauces and herbs to cover the rotting taste of old meat or fish. The Romans' favorite sauce was liquamen, which was strained from salted fish guts that had been left out in the sun.

In Rome many people did not cook at all, since ovens were banned in the crowded tenement buildings because of the risk of fires. Instead, people visited stalls and taverns to buy soup, sausages, pies, fried fish, and fruit.

▽ Many hosts saw a party as a great opportunity to show off their wealth and impress the guests with fine silverware.

The richest Romans held splendid dinner parties. Guests reclined on three couches around a table, supporting themselves with their left elbows and holding their food in their right hands. They rarely used knives or spoons, so the food served had to be easy to pick up and not too hot. The host's slaves served everyone, but guests sometimes brought their own slaves to help out.

▷ Guests at big banquets ate huge quantities of food. Salads and oysters were brought out for appetizers, followed by several courses of game birds, boar, venison, hare, ham, and fish. Meals ended with honey cakes and fruit. Sometimes guests made themselves vomit so that they could squeeze more food into their stomachs.

Shopping in Rome

Every day ships and wagons arrived in Rome from all over the empire, carrying goods made in distant corners of the world. Traders from as far as India and China brought luxury silks and spices to delight the wealthy buyers. The city's bustling markets and stores offered almost anything for sale, from basics such as grain, pots, and clothing to beautiful vases, skilled slaves, and elegant jewelry.

▷ Rome was the richest city in the empire, and luxury goods were plentiful. This vase, made out of blue-and-white glass, would have taken months to make and could only have been afforded by the very rich.

Most Roman stores were stalls or rooms opening out onto the street. The owners usually lived in the room above and pulled wooden shutters across the front to keep out thieves during the night. There was a wide variety of exotic things on sale: wool from Great Britain; silver from Spain; rugs from Turkey; and perfumes from Iran. The same currency was used across the whole empire, from Asia Minor to Great Britain, but goods were at their most expensive in Rome itself.

◁ Trajan's market near the forum was a huge semicircular shopping center carved out of the side of a hill, with 150 stores, offices, and a central open space where traders set up stalls.

▽ Most citizens only went shopping for expensive, unique items. Shopping for food and other essentials was done by male slaves.

▽ Slaves were brought in from conquered lands. Those who could cook, dance, or sing were worth much more money than those without any skills.

By far the most important thing on sale was grain—imported daily from Africa, since Italian farmers could not produce enough wheat to feed Rome by themselves. In hard times, the emperor gave free handouts of grain to the poor.

Homes

The city of Rome sprawled over seven hills. The richest people lived in spacious villas on the airy higher ground, while everyone else was crammed into ramshackle apartment buildings in the valleys below. In the summer these hot and overcrowded streets were breeding grounds for diseases, and the few who could afford to left the city to stay in the countryside.

▽ Buildings were arranged in blocks called insulae, meaning "islands," divided up by the grid of roads. In many places the streets were so narrow that it was possible to shake hands with someone in the building across the street.

◁ A fire in an insula spread quickly and was very dangerous. Rome had seven squads of professional firefighters, the *vigiles*. They also helped keep order in the rowdy streets.

Most of Rome's people lived in small rented rooms in large, crowded tenement buildings. These stuffy apartments were vulnerable to fires and were so badly made that they often fell down. Each block had up to six stories and had stores on the first floor. The noise of traders' carts kept people awake for most of the night, except for those who lived at the very top of the building.

▽ The atrium was the entrance hall, where wealthy families received their guests. It was brightly decorated, with painted walls, statues, and mosaic floors to impress visitors.

A rich man's house was built around the atrium, an open hall with a hole in the ceiling and a pool in the middle to catch rainwater. Doors to the dining room, living rooms, kitchen, and bedrooms were on the sides. The atrium was the house's main source of light and air—outside walls had few windows in order to keep out noise and burglars. At the back of the house was a peristyle, a garden filled with shrubs and statues.

△ Even big houses did not have much furniture. The couches in the dining room were the most important items. Adding a woolen blanket meant that they doubled up as beds at night.

▷ Many houses had small shrines where families worshiped their own personal gods, called lares. Every day they left offerings of wine, cakes, and incense at the shrines, which contained tiny statues of the lar. Offerings were supposed to bring wealth and happiness to the households.

The baths

The public baths were an essential part of life in Rome. People visited the baths to relax, swim, talk, and play games in magnificent surroundings. There were hundreds of baths in the city, and many people visited one every day. Most trips were free, because rich men paid everyone's fees in the hopes of gaining votes or increasing their popularity.

△ Romans cleaned themselves at the baths by rubbing oil into their skin and then scraping off the mingled oil and dirt with a blunt metal tool called a strigil.

▷ Water for the baths was heated by underground furnaces. This meant that the tiles on the floor could be scalding hot. Visitors wore sandals to protect their feet.

▽ Men and women bathed at separate times. A bell was rung to signal the changeover.

▽ The floors of baths were covered in intricate mosaics. This one from Pompeii shows an octopus surrounded by fish.

▽ All of the baths were very richly decorated. The rooms were lined with marble pillars, and the ceilings were high and beautifully painted. This luxury gave even poor people a regular taste of the power and wealth of Rome.

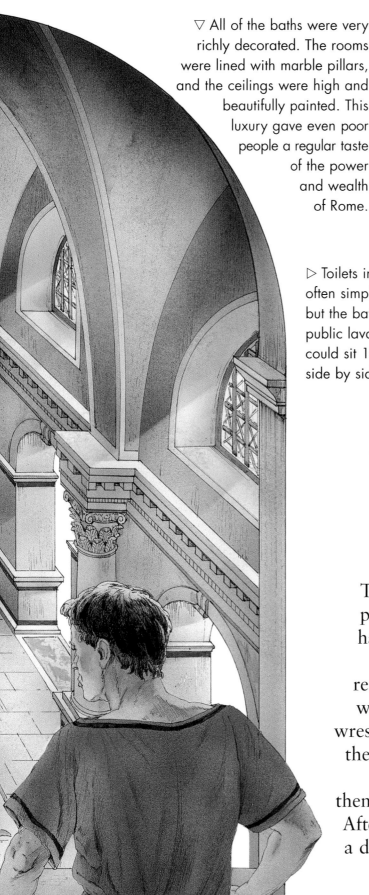

▷ Toilets in Roman homes were often simply pots in a corner, but the baths had splendid public lavatories. Some could sit 16 people side by side.

The baths included hot and cold pools, steam rooms, saunas, and hair salons. The largest ones also had forecourts with stores, restaurants, and libraries. Visitors warmed up in the gymnasium by wrestling or playing ball games and then bathed in the caldarium—the hottest room of all—to bring themselves out in a cleansing sweat. After a massage, they finished with a dip into an ice-cold plunge pool.

The theater

Visiting the theater was a favorite pastime. Semicircular stone theaters hosted plays and games, often to celebrate recent military victories. The Romans got their love of drama from the Greeks, but although some Greek tragedies were shown, most Romans preferred comedies. The action was fast, with lots of crude jokes and happy endings. Some characters were very popular—such as the cunning slave who always managed to talk himself out of trouble in the nick of time.

▽ Roman audiences were very noisy. If they were pleased, they clapped their hands, snapped their fingers and thumbs, and waved their togas. If not, they hissed, shouted, and made rude noises.

△ Actors rehearsed in a building behind the stage. Actors were all men, but they played women's roles too.

Romans loved special effects and big spectacles. Ghosts appeared through holes in the stage floor and winches helped produce gods from above. In some tragedies, a real-life criminal was brought onstage and executed. There was not much scenery, although real chariots and horses sometimes appeared onstage. Actors wore masks, wigs, and special colors that showed what type of character they were playing.

▽ Roman comedies usually had a lot of movement to keep the audience's attention, with characters chasing each other, falling over, or performing gymnastics.

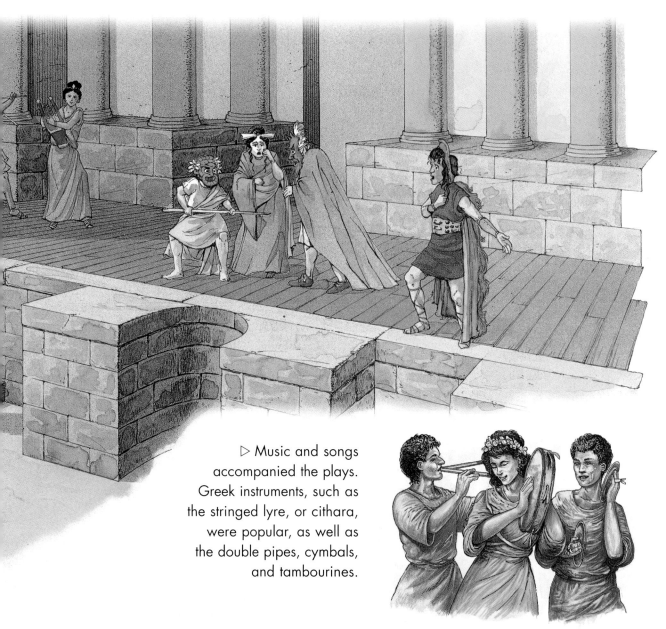

▷ Music and songs accompanied the plays. Greek instruments, such as the stringed lyre, or cithara, were popular, as well as the double pipes, cymbals, and tambourines.

Circus Maximus

Chariot racing was the most popular sport in Rome, and in the time of Hadrian, the Circus Maximus was the biggest stadium in the world. Up to 250,000 people could crowd in to see the races—more than one half of the city's population! Citizens supported one of the four teams: the Blues, Whites, Reds, or Greens. Entry was free to watch all 24 races in one day.

△ Betting on chariot races and gladiator fights was allowed, but all other gambling was illegal. Many Romans went to secret betting houses, where they could wager money on dice or the toss of a coin.

△ Cheating was common. Drivers sometimes slipped a stick through their rivals' spokes to make them crash.

The race began when an official dropped a handkerchief. There were seven 1-mi. (1.5-km) laps of the spina, or wall, in the middle of the arena. On top of the spina there were seven metal dolphins— one was removed to mark each lap.

△ Chariot races were popular with both rich and poor Romans. Children from wealthy families had small chariots to play in, pulled by donkeys or goats.

Chariots were light and easy to maneuver, but they were also flimsy and could easily overturn. The most dangerous parts of the course were the corners, where drivers had to turn at high speeds. Collisions were common as drivers tried to force opponents into the wall. Each driver tied the reins around his waist so that he had his hands free to whip the horses. This meant that if he crashed, he could easily be dragged to his death.

The Colosseum

On public holidays, citizens enjoyed watching savage blood sports in the Colosseum. This was the biggest amphitheater in the empire and hosted spectacular and extremely violent entertainment. There was everything from mock sea battles to public executions, with slaves and criminals being eaten alive by wild beasts.

△ Exotic animals were imported from all over the world. They were usually killed in huge mock hunting displays. However, ferocious lions were often used to devour helpless criminals.

◁ Trained fighters called gladiators were prisoners, slaves, or criminals. If they entertained the crowd, they received gifts of coins, but only those who survived many fights were set free. These lucky few were given bone tablets with their names on them to prove that they were free men.

The Colosseum had 80 entrances so that people could find seats quickly. There was also a canvas awning that could be pulled over the top to protect spectators from the sun. This was operated by teams of slaves who pulled ropes outside. Underneath there were underground chambers for the gladiators and animals.

Gladiator fights were the most popular form of entertainment in the Colosseum. There were several different types of fighters, each with their own weapons and armor. Most fights were to the death, but a beaten gladiator could appeal to the emperor to save his life. If he had fought bravely, the emperor gave a thumbs-up to let him live. If not, a thumbs-down was the signal for his opponent to kill him.

▽ The nimble retiarius had a net to snare his enemy and a trident to stab him. The secutor was heavily armored, making him powerful but slow.

▽ Heavy helmets offered protection, but they were difficult to see out of. This was a serious disadvantage against fast opponents.

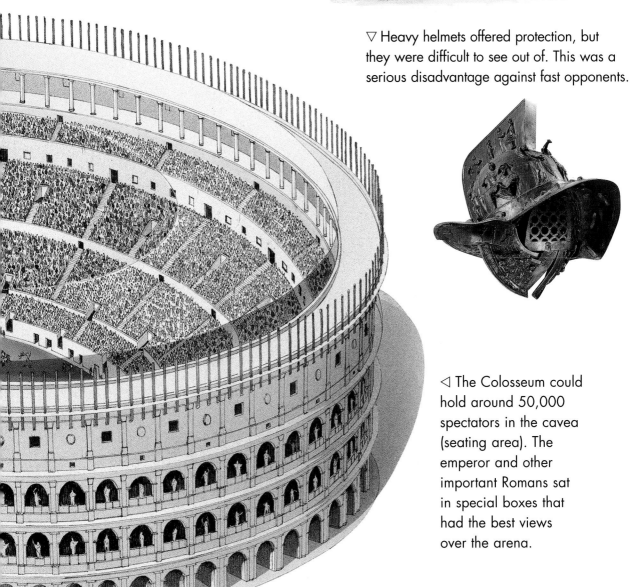

◁ The Colosseum could hold around 50,000 spectators in the cavea (seating area). The emperor and other important Romans sat in special boxes that had the best views over the arena.

Temples and worship

Romans believed in many different gods. They thought that everything from personal health to success in war depended on the gods' favor and that regular rituals had to be carried out in order to keep them satisfied. In hundreds of temples across the city, priests elected from among the nobles performed sacrifices on behalf of the people. Festivals and feast days were held for each god, and offerings of fruit, wine, and animals were made every day.

◁ Jupiter was the king of the gods, and Rome itself was thought to be under his protection. The Romans had gods to watch over every aspect of their lives. Some of the most important were Mars, the god of war; Apollo, the god of light and music; Vesta, the goddess of the home and the hearth; and Minerva, the goddess of wisdom.

▷ Hadrian built a great temple to all of the gods—the Pantheon. It was a masterpiece of engineering, with a huge dome and statues of the gods lining the walls. The oculus, a single hole at the top, provided light and represented the sun.

▽ Priests often sacrificed animals to the gods. The more willingly they went to the slaughter, the better the omen. Once dead, the entrails were studied. If they were in good condition, the animal was cooked and eaten.

▽ People who were sick would pray to the gods for help. In addition to praying, they would leave a gift at the temple, which was usually a model of the diseased part of their body.

The Romans looked to the gods whenever they had an important decision to make. Thunder, lightning, and the behavior of birds were studied by special priests called augurs, who looked for omens—signs from the gods—that would tell them what was going to happen in the future.

The countryside

Although Rome was the capital of the empire, the Italian countryside surrounding it was also important. For the rich, it provided a refuge from the chaos of the city. Vast farming estates of wealthy families supplied most of the food that kept Rome going, as well as plenty of wine and olive oil. These products were carried in huge quantities to ports on the Mediterranean coast and exported by sea all over the empire.

▽ Merchant ships were heavy and slow. They each had a square sail and two big steering oars at the stern. Oil and wine were carried in large pottery jars called amphorae.

◁ Only 15.5 mi. (25km) from the city at the mouth of the Tiber river was Rome's great port of Ostia. Huge warehouses on the seafront stored grain, wine, and olive oil before barges brought them up the river and into Rome.

▽ Most rich families only visited the estates in the summer to get out of the sweltering city. But there was a work force of slaves on the farms all year round who tended the crops and livestock.

At the heart of a farming estate was the nobleman's villa, surrounded by vineyards and houses for slaves and workers. In the fall, slaves picked the grapes and crushed them to extract the juice. This was poured into large, half-buried jars to ferment and become wine. The jars were sealed with pitch to keep out rain. Poor-quality grapes were made into wine for the workers.

△ When the olives had been harvested from the trees, they were piled inside an olive press. Slaves pulled down the handles to squash the olives and squeeze out the oil into jars.

The countryside was crisscrossed with gigantic aqueducts running to Rome from distant water sources. They supplied more than 47 million gal. (180 million L) of water to the city every day, mostly to baths and fountains. The water moved by gravity, so each aqueduct was angled downhill along its entire length. Stone slabs covered the water channel to keep out any dirt.

Living in Rome

Life in Rome was hard for all but the very rich. Laws were enforced with tough punishments, and citizens were expected to obey a rigid social hierarchy. Those who got sick or were injured went to see doctors who had little scientific knowledge. Often there was not enough food for the poor.

◁ Magistrates were one of the few officials to be elected by Rome's citizens. These rich men spent a huge amount of money on pleasing the people and winning their support.

Medicine was based largely on herbal remedies and was not always effective. For broken ribs, for example, the writer Pliny recommended applying a mix of goat's dung and wine to the wound.

Roman society followed a very strict hierarchy. At the top were Roman citizens, who were divided into the wealthy nobility and the ordinary people, or plebians. Noncitizens from outside Rome had fewer rights. Below all of these people were the slaves, who did most of the work on the farms and in the city and had almost no rights at all.

△ Surgeons had sophisticated tools to operate on wounds and broken bones, but the only painkillers were poppy juice and wine.

▽ Four squads of special legionaries were assigned to carry out police duties in Rome. In times of serious disturbance, the Praetorian Guard was called in.

The Romans were enthusiastic about discipline and dealt with criminals severely. Minor crimes were punished by beatings. Thieves were branded. For the worst offenses, slaves could be executed by crucifixion. An elite force of legionaries, the Praetorian Guard, had the job of protecting the emperor. No other legions were allowed close to Rome so that the emperor could not be overthrown.

The emperor appointed the most important officials, who were all nobles. Rich young men became lawyers and magistrates before being appointed as governors of faraway regions of the empire.

◁ Some slaves were made to wear special tags with their master's name and address on them. If they ran away, the slaves could be caught and returned.

29

Quiz

At its height, Rome was the most vibrant and exciting city in the ancient world. Try this quiz to find out how much you can remember about life in Rome. Answers can be found on page 32.

1. The forum was one of the oldest parts of Rome. How did it first start out?

a) As a hilltop fortress.

b) As a marketplace in a village.

c) As a temple to Romulus, the founder of Rome.

2. What creature took care of Romulus as a baby?

a) A wolf.

b) A bear.

c) An eagle.

3. What was most likely to keep people awake at night in the streets of Rome?

a) Traders' carts bringing goods into the city.

b) All-night chariot races through the streets.

c) Drunken revelers.

4. What did Roman women make wigs out of?

a) Horse hair from Arabian stallions.

b) Human hair from slaves.

c) Finely spun silk from the Far East.

5. Why would a Roman woman want to have a pale face?

a) It proved that she was of pure Roman blood.

b) It was thought to be a sign of good health.

c) It proved that she was rich enough to stay indoors and not do any work.

6. Goods came to Rome from all over the empire. What was the most vital import?

a) Swords brought from Asia Minor.

b) Grain imported from Africa.

c) Tea from Great Britain.

7. What was liquamen?

a) A mix of rotting fish guts and salt that the Romans used as a sauce.

b) A strong alcoholic drink that was made from cranberries.

c) A mix of boars' droppings and wine used to treat bad chest injuries.

8. A retiarius was one of the most popular types of gladiators. What kind of weapons did he carry?

a) A net and a trident.

b) A short sword and a heavy rectangular shield.

c) A light javelin and a round shield.

9. The lares were very important to most Romans. Who were they?

a) Rome's special firefighters.

b) The chief priests of Jupiter who worked at the Pantheon.

c) Household gods who watched over families.

10. How did charioteers know how many laps were left in the Circus Maximus?

a) A track marshal waved a flag with a number written on it.

b) They had to remember themselves.

c) The laps were counted with metal dolphins.

11. Romans loved going to the theater. What type of play did they like to see the most?

a) Greek tragedies, with plenty of death and sorrow.

b) Fast-paced comedies, with lots of farcical situations and silly jokes.

c) Political satires, filled with angry jokes at the emperor's expense.

Index

Acknowledgments

Inklink Firenze illustrators
Simone Boni, Alessandro Rabatti, Lorenzo Pieri, Luigi Critone, Lucia Mattioli, Francisco Petracchi, Theo Caneschi, Federico Ferniani, Alain Bressan, Concetta D'Amato.

Additional illustrations
Richard Berridge, Luigi Galante, Nicki Palin, Thomas Troyer.

Picture credits
b = bottom, c = center, l = left, r = right, t = top
4cl The Bridgeman Art Library, London/New York/Museo Archeologico Nazionale, Naples; 6cl AKG London/Erich Lessing; 9tr The British Museum; c Scala; 11tr The Bridgeman Art Library, London/New York/Louvre, Paris, France; 12c Ancient Art & Architecture; 15br The British Museum; 17tr Ancient Art & Architecture; 19tl Ancient Art & Architecture;

20bl C. M. Dixon/British Museum; 23tl Giraudon/Louvre, Paris; 25cr AKG London/Museum für Deutsche Geschichte, Berlin; 27cr AKG London/Erich Lessing; 28br Scala

The publisher would like to thank the following for permission to reproduce their material. Every care has been taken to trace copyright holders. However, if there have been unintentional omissions or failure to trace copyright holders, we apologize and will, if informed, endeavor to make corrections in any future edition.

Quiz answers

1. **b)**   2. **a)**   3. **a)**   4. **b)**   5. **c)**   6. **b)**   7. **a)**   8. **a)**   9. **c)**   10. **c)**   11. **b)**